Life Span Development Laboratory Manual

SIXTH EDITION

Editors:
Barbara Lusk
Aimee Johnson

Contributing Authors:
William Adler
Roberta Benavides
Martha Ellis
Aimee Johnson
Dan Lipscomb
Barbara Lusk
Jennifer Brooks
Marti Weaver
Debbie White

Collin County Community College

Printed in the United States of America.

ISBN: 1-933005-73-4

59 Damonte Ranch Parkway, #B 284 • Reno, NV 89521 • (800) 970-1883

www.benttreepress.com

Address all correspondence and order information to the above address.

TO THE STUDENT:

Welcome to Life Span Psychology. Whether you are planning a career in psychology, teaching, nursing, education, sociology or taking this course to gain more insight into how people grow and develop throughout their lives, we hope you will find this a useful and exciting course.

This laboratory manual contains a variety of activities related to pertinent research. The laboratory component of this course was designed to provide you with experiences to enhance your understanding of the different stages of the human life span. Through this understanding, we hope you will gain a greater appreciation of yourself, others, and the world around you.

TABLE OF CONTENTS

UNIT 1 – INTRODUCTION   PAGE

UNIT 2 – INFANCY

UNIT 3 – EARLY CHILDHOOD

UNIT 4 – LATE CHILDHOOD

UNIT 5 – ADOLESCENCE

UNIT 6 – EARLY ADULTHOOD

UNIT 7 – MIDDLE ADULTHOOD

UNIT 8 – LATE ADULTHOOD

REFERENCES

Introduction

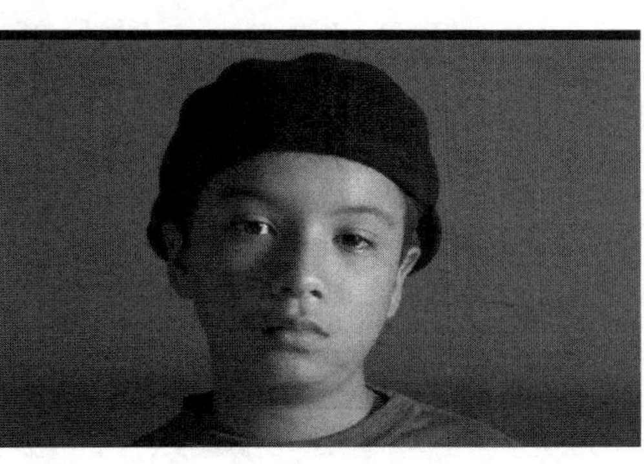

ANALYSIS OF A POPULAR ARTICLE

You are to choose a popular magazine article related to life span development

Materials: Current popular magazines

Procedure: Read the article and write a typed, double-spaced (two page minimum) paper which will include the information below.

1. Summarize the information contained in the article

2. Evaluate the information in the article:
    a. How were the facts supporting the author's claims derived? Were sources of information cited?
    b. Did the author's conclusions follow logically from these facts? Were there alternative explanations?
    c. What future research can be suggested by these findings?

3. Based on your evaluation, rate the article as excellent (based on sound research), average (research is not extensive), or poor (little research data to support claims). Explain your rating.

ATTITUDES SURVEY

One of the methods used by developmental psychologists to understand growth and change is the survey method. In this approach, information is collected in numerical form (usually from a representative sample of a larger population) and analyzed.

In this experiment you will be researching people's attitudes on a variety of developmental issues.

Materials: Surveys on the following pages of your manual

Procedure: You are to ask 3 people from each age group to answer this survey. These people must be from 4 different stages (age groups) of development. The stages are: adolescence (11-22), early adulthood (22-40), middle adulthood (40-65), and late adulthood (65+).

Ask each person to fill out the survey as honestly as possible. This survey is anonymous. The respondents should only place their age at the top of the page. Clarify the meaning of the statements, but try not to influence attitudes if they have questions.

Answer the questions on your Laboratory Report Forms(s).

Turn in all 12 surveys and your report form. Make additional copies of the survey to complete the assignment.

ATTITUDES SURVEY

Please choose the response that most clearly indicates your opinion in most circumstances.

Strongly Agree	Agree	Uncertain	Disagree	Strongly Disagree
1	**2**	**3**	**4**	**5**

1.   Love lasts forever.

    1   2   3   4   5

2.   Marriage should be "till death do us part."

    1   2   3   4   5

3.   It is all right for a man and woman to live together outside of marriage.

    1   2   3   4   5

4.   Love relationships should be heterosexual only.

    1   2   3   4   5

5.   It is okay for men to have extra-marital affairs.

    1   2   3   4   5

6.   It is okay for women to have extra-marital affairs.

    1   2   3   4   5

7.   Women should usually obtain custody of the children in a divorce settlement.

    1   2   3   4   5

8.   Day care centers are a suitable substitute for parenting in the home.

    1   2   3   4   5

9.   Television is an influence on our children's education.

    1   2   3   4   5

ATTITUDES SURVEY – CONT.

10.   Public schools are doing a good job education our children.

    1   2   3   4   5

11.   Sex education should be taught in the public school system.

    1   2   3   4   5

12.   It is important to teach children a belief in a supreme being.

    1   2   3   4   5

13.   Parents do not have to explain reasons of punishment to children.

    1   2   3   4   5

14.   It is acceptable for women to have full-time careers.

    1   2   3   4   5

15.   Salaries should be equal for men and women.

    1   2   3   4   5

16.   Most adults are satisfied with the career in which they are employed.

    1   2   3   4   5

17.   Retirement should not be based on age but on capabilities.

    1   2   3   4   5

18.   Senility is a natural development in older adults.

    1   2   3   4   5

19.   My age is:

    11-22   22-40   40-65   65+

20.   My sex is:

    Male   female

LABORATORY REPORT FORM: ATTITUDES SURVEY

Summary:

1. What questions had similar responses by all of your subjects?

2. What questions had drastically different responses by your subjects?

3. Did you see any differences in opinion that you would attribute to age differences of your subjects? Explain with examples.

4. Did you see any differences in opinion that you would attribute to the sex differences of your subjects? Explain with examples.

5. What conclusions did you draw from the results of this survey?

THE CONTEXT OF DEVELOPMENT

Dr. Bronfenbrenner stresses the importance of understanding the context of development. His ecological theory of development separates these contexts into systems: microsystem, mesosystem, exosystem, macrosystem and chronosystem.

Materials: Paper and pencil

Procedures: You are to work in small groups, writing a one to two page original scenario which depicts a day in the life of an individual (you select the age, sex, setting, time frame). This scenario must include events that represent each of Bronfenbrenner's systems. Present your scenario to the class. Students will be asked to identify the different systems represented in your example.

Answer the questions on your Laboratory Report Form(s).

LABORATORY REPORT FORM:
THE CONTEXT OF DEVELOPMENT

Summary:

1.   Identify each system in your scenario.

2.   Describe the interplay between an individual's genetic predispositions and the person's environment.

Infancy

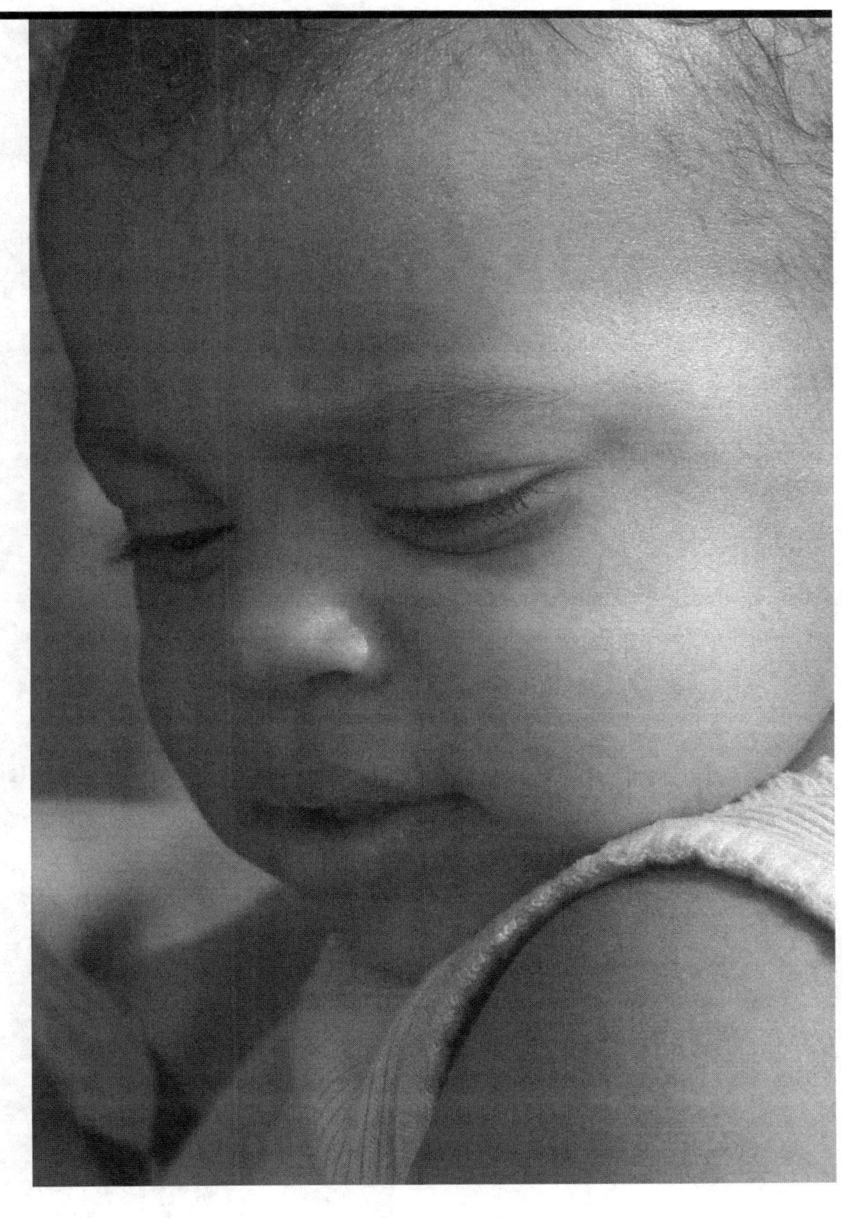

OBSERVATION: INFANCY

One of the best ways to learn about people is to observe them in the real world. This will give you the opportunity to see the full, genuine, and dynamic quality of human life across the life span.

Materials: Paper and pen for note-taking

Procedure: You will be observing people from **birth through two years of age**. You will be watching and recording behaviors. You are to observe each of the six stages of life span development for two hours, equaling a total of 12 hours for the entire semester. The two hour requirement for each stage does not have to be done in one sitting or with only one person. In fact, shorter segments with a variety of people are strongly encouraged so that you see individual differences as well as developmental similarities within the stage. The combinations need to total 2 hours. While observing, take notes and then consolidate your data into specific information for your paper. The format for this paper is described below.

A FEW HINTS FOR OBSERVING PEOPLE

1.   Be as unobtrusive as possible. You are entering the subjects' world so please do not disturb this world. Try to be objective.

2.   All you need is paper and pen to write down a few notes about the behavior and people you are observing. Do not take recorders or cameras. Do not write continually – observe, watch, listen.

3.   Write up your observation as soon as you finish observing while it is still fresh in your memory. Details are important. If you happen to know any of the subjects, do not use names when you write your observation.

4.   Observe in natural settings: parks, restaurants, malls, sports events, your front yard, schools, etc.

5.   Have the purpose of your research firmly in mind. Will you watch the entire playground or pick out one child to watch? Will you focus on one type of behavior or record all activities?

6.   Review developmental milestones from various theories before beginning your observation.

7.   Record verbal and nonverbal communication. Words, cries, screams, smiles, gestures, frowns, etc. all are important.

8.   If anyone asks what you are doing, be truthful.

OBSERVATION INFANCY – CONT.

FORMAT FOR THE OBSERVATION PAPER

Your paper must be typed, double-spaced, and a minimum of two pages in length. Indicate the location of the observation, the approximate age of subjects and the sex of subjects. The first section of the paper should be devoted to specific, objective behavioral data. The second section of the paper should emphasize the connections between your observations and developmental concepts from your text.

LANGUAGE DEVELOPMENT

Children of different ages respond differently in tasks of linguistic ability. One of the aspects of developmental psychology is the study of how and when changes in language occur. Certain syntactical styles develop at specific developmental stages. In this experiment you will attempt to see the language rules applicable to 2 year olds.

Materials: Laboratory Report Form

Procedure: Ask a child as near to 2 years of age as possible to help you with this project. You might tell him/her that you will be playing a game of "you say what I say."

Read each of the following sentences on the Laboratory Report Form to the child and record exactly what the child says when he/she tries to repeat after you. Spell phonetically if you need to. (Example: "red" may be said as "wed")

Answer the questions on your Laboratory Report Form(s).

LABORATORY REPORT FORM: LANGUAGE DEVELOPMENT

1.   The round ball is red.

     ____

     ____

2.   Horses can eat grass.

     ____

     ____

3.   The pretty lady is wearing a blue dress.

     ____

     ____

4.   Where is the rope?

     ____

     ____

5.   Daddy is too big.

     ____

     ____

6.   The happy fat man walked fast.

     ____

     ____

7.   Yesterday was a very hot day.

     ____

     ____

8.   The little boy is in the truck.

     ____

     ____

LANGUAGE DEVELOPMENT – CONT.

9.   The girl whom we met today laughed loudly.

____

____

10.   I am a good girl/boy.

____

____

Summary:

1. What kinds of words in the adult sentences did the child repeat?

2. What words were omitted from the sentences by the child?

3. What conclusions can you reach about language ability in children from these responses?

OBJECT PERMANENCE

Object permanence is the cognitive characteristic that an object continues to exist when it is outside the perceptual field. As adults, we take this ability for granted. Infants (before the age of about 6 to 9 months) do not necessarily understand object permanence. During the sensorimotor stage of cognitive development, infants acquire an understanding of this concept.

In this experiment you will be determining whether or not an infant has acquired object permanence.

Materials: A small stuffed animal, rattle or other toy appropriate for young infant.

Procedure: You will need to visit an infant around 4 to 5 months of age. After you have made friends with the baby, offer the infant the stuffed animal or other toy. Let the infant play with the toy for a few minutes and then gently remove the toy. As the infant watches, hide the toy behind a pillow or under a blanket. Record the baby's responses on the laboratory report form.

Repeat this same procedure with an infant around 9 to 12 months of age. Record the baby's responses.

Note: When you observe an infant, be sure to discuss with the parents what you are doing and what you have learned. Parents sometimes worry about what you have found out about their children. Be sure to say something reassuring about their child and let them know you are not here to criticize them or their child. The parents are taking a risk by letting you study their child. Show your appreciation and give encouragement to the parents.

Answer the questions on your Laboratory Report Form(s).

LABORATORY REPORT FORM:
OBJECT PERMANENCE

Infant #1 (4 to 5 months)

1.   What did the baby do when you hid the toy? Record all behavior.

2.   Has this infant developed the concept of object permanence? How do you know?

LABORATORY REPORT FORM:
OBJECT PERMANENCE

Infant #2 (9 to 12 months)

3.   What did the baby do when you hid the toy? Record all behavior.

4.   Has this infant developed the concept of object permanence? How do you know?

LITERATURE ANALYSIS

In this assignment you will be examining samples of children's literature. Specifically, you will be studying how children's literature influences gender role and gender identity development in early and late childhood.

Remember that gender roles are social-cognitive principles prescribing and regulating the behavior of the sexes. Gender identity is the personal identity as a woman or a man which derives from assimilating gender role principles.

Masculine and feminine characteristics are learned and reinforced through a complex system of socially based sanctions externally applied and internalized by the individual. This process starts at infancy and goes through adulthood with children beginning to understand gender-appropriate behavior during the preschool years.

Materials: 2 fairy tales and 2 current children's stories or 1 children's book (a minimum of 100 pages in length) and 2 fairy tales.

Procedure: You are to read 2 classic children's fairy tales such as <u>Cinderella</u>, <u>Hansel & Gretel</u>, <u>Little Red Riding Hood</u>, <u>Rapunzel</u>, etc.

Next you are to read 2 current children's short stories such as <u>Steven Kellogg's Best Friends</u> or <u>Pinkerton</u>, <u>Behave</u>; any selection from the <u>Berenstain Bears</u> series; Sendak's <u>Where the Wild Things Are</u>; Hurd's <u>I Dance in My Red Pajamas</u>; Shirley Hughes' <u>Moving Molly</u>.

Or

You may read 1 current children's book (<u>Ramona</u> series, <u>Anastasia</u> series, etc.).

Compare the two short stories or the book to the classic fairy tales.

Answer the questions on your Laboratory Report Form(s).

Copy forms as needed.

LABORATORY REPORT FORM: LITERATURE ANALYSIS

Story Title ____

1.   How many male characters are portrayed?

2.   How many female characters are portrayed?

3.   What roles did the males provide?

4.   What roles did the females provide?

5.   How is masculinity portrayed both positively and negatively?

6.   How is femininity portrayed both positively and negatively?

7.   What is portrayed as appropriate female behavior?

8.   What is portrayed as appropriate male behavior?

LABORATORY REPORT FORM: LITERATURE ANALYSIS

9.   How do women relate to each other and to men?

10.   How do men relate to each other and to women?

11.   How do men solve problems?

12.   How do women solve problems?

13.   What emotions do men experience?

14.   What emotions do women experience?

15.   Is there competition between people or cooperation for development of the individual?

16.   How many older adults were in the story? How were they portrayed?

LABORATORY REPORT FORM: LITERATURE ANALYSIS

Story Title ____

1.   How many male characters are portrayed?

2.   How many female characters are portrayed?

3.   What roles did the males provide?

4.   What roles did the females provide?

5.   How is masculinity portrayed both positively and negatively?

6.   How is femininity portrayed both positively and negatively?

7.   What is portrayed as appropriate female behavior?

8.   What is portrayed as appropriate male behavior?

LABORATORY REPORT FORM: LITERATURE ANALYSIS

9.   How do women relate to each other and to men?

10.   How do men relate to each other and to women?

11.   How do men solve problems?

12.   How do women solve problems?

13.   What emotions do men experience?

14.   What emotions do women experience?

15.   Is there competition between people or cooperation for development of the individual?

16.   How many older adults were in the story? How were they portrayed?

LABORATORY REPORT FORM: LITERATURE ANALYSIS

Summary:

1. How is masculinity portrayed in the classic fairy tales?

2. How is femininity portrayed in the classic fairy tales?

3. How is the male portrayed in the current literature?

4. How is the female portrayed in the current literature?

5. Were there significant differences in these portrayals? Explain.

6. Describe the effects of literature upon a child's gender-role development.

Early Childhood

OBSERVATION: EARLY CHILDHOOD

One of the best ways to learn about people is to observe them in the real world. This will give you the opportunity to see the full, genuine, and dynamic quality of human life across the life span.

Materials: Paper and pen for note-taking

Procedure: You will be observing people from **three through seven years of age**. You will be watching and recording behaviors. You are to observe each of the six stages of life span development for two hours, equaling a total of 12 hours for the entire semester. The two hour requirement for each stage does not have to be done in one sitting or with only one person. In fact, shorter segments with a variety of people are strongly encouraged so that you see individual differences as well as developmental similarities within the stage. The combinations need to total 2 hours. While observing, take notes and then consolidate your data into specific information for your paper. The format for this paper is described below.

A FEW HINTS FOR OBSERVING PEOPLE

1.   Be as unobtrusive as possible. You are entering the subjects' world so please do not disturb this world. Try to be objective.

2.   All you need is paper and pen to write down a few notes about the behavior and people you are observing. Do not take recorders or cameras. Do not write continually – observe, watch, listen.

3.   Write up your observation as soon as you finish observing while it is still fresh in your memory. Details are important. If you happen to know any of the subjects, do not use names when you write your observation.

4.   Observe in natural settings: parks, restaurants, malls, sports events, your front yard, schools, etc.

5.   Have the purpose of your research firmly in mind. Will you watch the entire playground or pick out one child to watch? Will you focus on one type of behavior or record all activities?

6.   Review developmental milestones from various theories before beginning your observation.

7.   Record verbal and nonverbal communication. Words, cries, screams, smiles, gestures, frowns, etc. all are important.

8.   If anyone asks what you are doing, be truthful.

OBSERVATION EARLY CHILDHOOD – CONT.

FORMAT FOR THE OBSERVATION PAPER

Your paper must be typed, double-spaced, and a minimum of two pages in length. Indicate the location of the observation, the approximate age of subjects and the sex of subjects. The first section of the paper should be devoted to specific, objective behavioral data. The second section of the paper should emphasize the connections between your observations and developmental concepts from your text.

EGOCENTRISM IN CHILDREN

Purpose: To demonstrate differences in egocentrism of children in preoperational (2-7 years) and concrete operational (7-11 years) stages.

Materials: Data Sheet
Drawings

Background: Egocentrism is a self-centered approach to the world which includes an inability to perceive the world and oneself through the eyes of other people. In older children and adults this is a negative characteristic and one that can be quite disconcerting. In young children from 2-6 years of age, it is normal behavior. In fact, young children cannot see the world otherwise, according to Piaget. Children see themselves as being at the center of the universe. They see the world in terms of their own actions and intentions toward the world and cannot perceive things from any viewpoint other than their own.

Children cannot imagine what a room looks like from where you are sitting. They may know they have 2 brothers and 1 sister, but they do not realize how many children their parents have. When they close their eyes they assume that since they cannot see you, then you must not be able to see them, either.

Procedure: You will need 2 children for this experiment, one between the ages of 2-6 (preferably 4 or younger, if possible) and one 7-11 years. You will test them on 3 tasks measuring egocentrism. In each case the child will be asked to view the world through another perspective. We would expect large differences in the ability of the 2 children in accomplishing these tasks.

EGOCENTRISM – CONT.

Task 1   Show the child the drawing of the doll sitting at the table. Ask the child to pick out from the 6 scenes below the drawing that represents what the doll sees from its position (position "A" at the table). Record the answer on the data sheet. Similarly require the child to state what scene is correct from table position B and C and record the answers on the data sheet. Follow this same procedure for the dog looking in the sandbox and record the answers. Do this for both of your subjects.

Task 2   Ask both children how many brothers and sisters they have. Record the answer. Then ask the children how many children their parents have. Record the answers for both children on the data sheet.

Task 3   Ask the child to close his/her eyes. Ask the child if he/she thinks you (the experimenter) can see the child while his/her eyes are closed. Record the answer on the data sheet.

EGOCENTRISM DATA SHEET

Task 1 – Pictures

Scene	Position	Child's Response Young	Older	Correct Response
Doll/Table	A	_____	_____	5
Doll/Table	B	_____	_____	6
Doll/Table	C	_____	_____	3
Dog/Sandbox	A	_____	_____	6
Dog/Sandbox	B	_____	_____	1
Dog/Sandbox	C	_____	_____	2
Total Correct		_____	_____	

Task 2 – Number of Siblings

	Child's Response Young	Older
How many brothers/sisters?	_____	_____
How may children do your parents have?	_____	_____

Task 3 – Eyes Closed

	Child's Response Young	Older
Can experimenter see the child?	_____	_____

EGOCENTRISM DATA SHEET – CONT.
Summary:

1.   On the basis of your data, would you conclude the young child was egocentric? Why or why not?

2.   Would you conclude the older subject was egocentric? Why or why not?

3.   Do you believe a child loses his/her egocentrism gradually or fairly suddenly? Explain your answer and justify it.

4.   Piaget feels developmental maturity must occur before a child becomes non-egocentric. What other factors might account for an older child being able to perform better on these tasks?

5.   What factors might contribute to adults maintaining a significant level of egocentrism?

Egocentrism Drawings

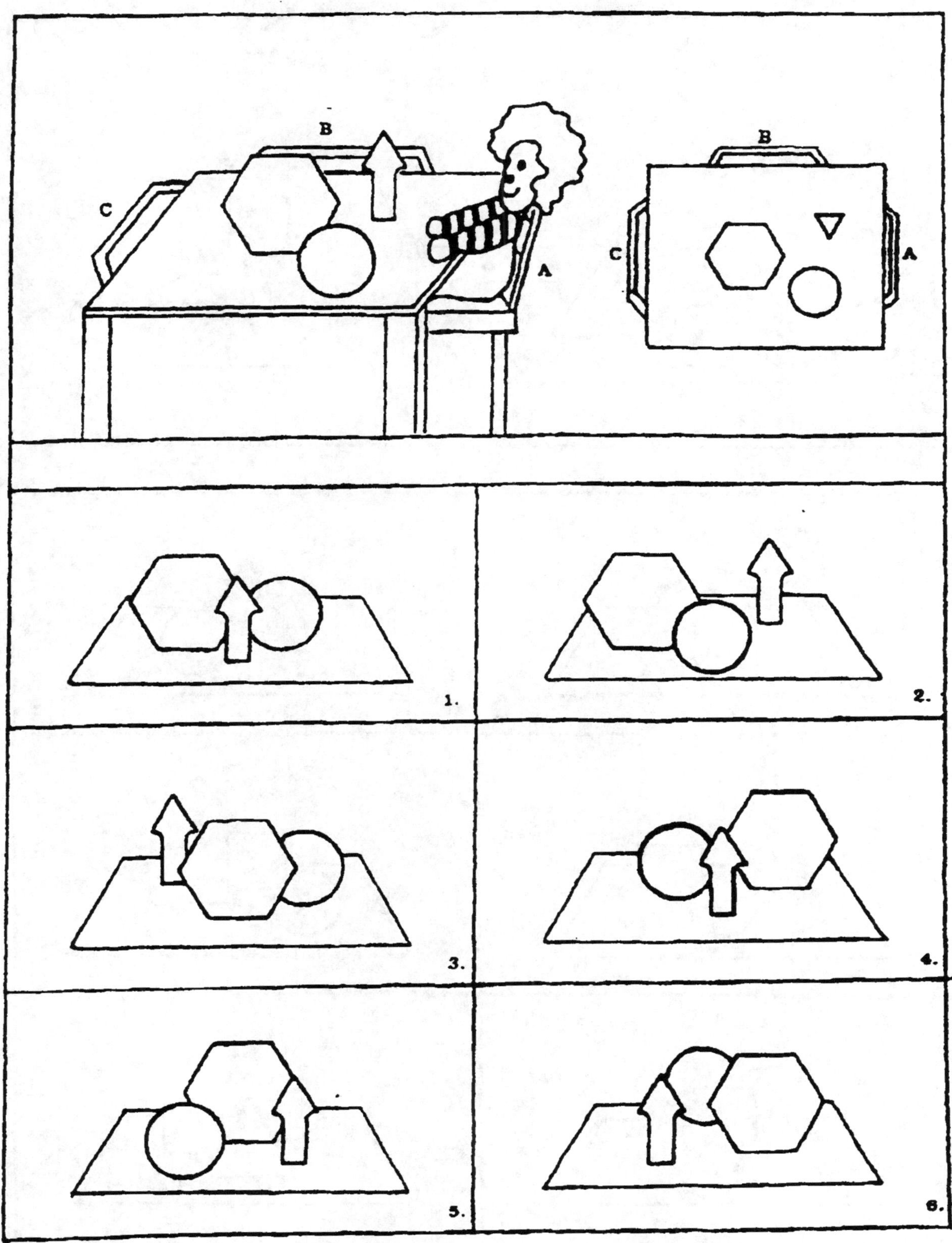

Egocentrism Drawings

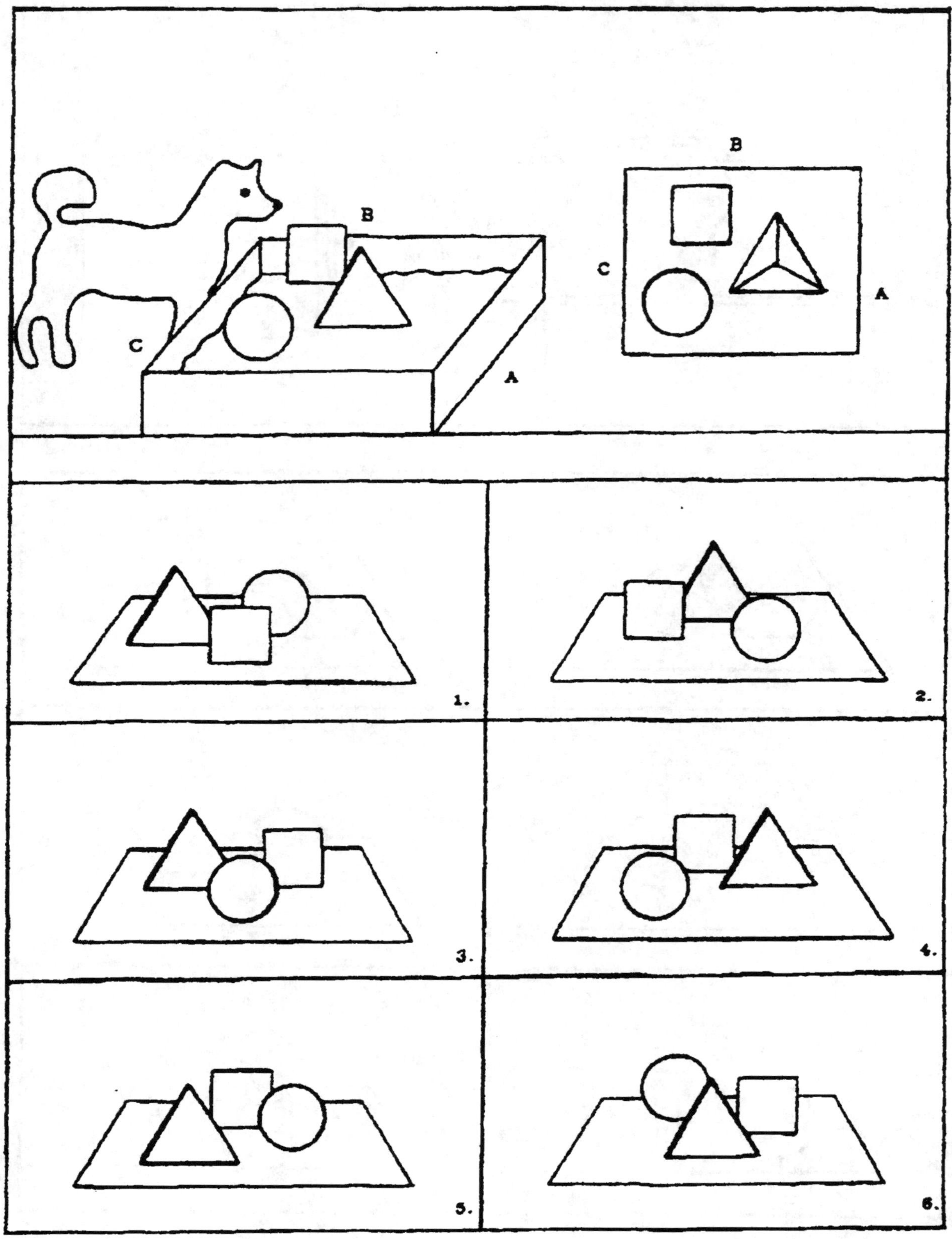

SHOW AND TELL

The topic of developmental psychology frequently generates a desire to share personal experiences. This activity allows for a formal way to integrate such discussion into the classroom by having you present a part of your childhood to the class.

Materials: Artifacts

Procedure: Bring some physical artifact from early childhood to class. (Example: a baby picture, a toy, an early craft project, etc.)

Think about how your artifact relates to a developmental concept that has been discussed in class or in the textbook and be prepared to briefly present that relationship.

Answer the questions on your Laboratory Report Form(s).

LABORATORY REPORT FORM:
SHOW AND TELL

Summary:

1.   How are artifacts used in psychological research in general?

2.   What inferences can a psychologist make about your current stage of development by simply examining your room?

3.   As you listen to other classmates' presentations, do you notice any commonalities or significant differences? Please elaborate.

CHILDREN'S APPERCEPTION TEST

The Children's Apperception Test, a projective psychological test, was designed to facilitate an understanding of a child's relationship to his/her most important figures and drives. The subject is shown a series of cards and is asked to tell a story about each. The examiner then interprets these responses using specific test criteria.

Materials: Children's Apperception Test
Transcript of a subject's responses

Procedure: You will be shown a series of pictures and will read the transcript of the anonymous subject's responses to each of these pictures. Choose four of the subject's stories to analyze using your laboratory report form.

Answer the questions on your Laboratory Report Form(s).

CHILDREN'S APPERCEPTION TEST TRANSCRIPT

Subject (S):   6 year old female

Experimenter (E):   We are going to play a game. I'm going to show you several pictures and I would like you to tell me a story about each picture. The story should have a beginning, middle, and end. Also, please tell me how the characters are feeling and what they are doing.

Subject interrupts

Experimenter: Yes, do have a question?

Subject: Do you tell the story first, or do you tell what the animals are doing and what's happening in the picture?

E: Your story should include what the animals are doing and what is happening in the picture. Are you ready to begin?

S: Yes.

E: Picture number one.

S: One day three baby chickens were eating porridge and the mother hen was watching them or should I say standing by. Then one of them got up and said, "I'm going to go out into the meadow." The others said, "We'll join you after we finish." Then the mother hen said to the one who was named Billy who wanted to go out in the field...and she said, "Wait for me and would you please wait for the others?" Then Billy sat down and waited.

E: Anything else?

S: and then the other two finished...and the mother hen said, "I'll be out on the front porch watching." So they all went and played some games. Can I say the end?

E: You bet!

S: The end.

E: Are you ready for picture 2?

S: Yes. Three bears were playing tug-a-war one day and there was one on one team and two on the other.   Then one of 'em stopped and they said I wanna play another game. So the other two stopped and before they started to play the new game, the mother asked, "Who won?" The daddy bear said, "I think we should say that it was a tie." So they went on to the next game. All they had to play with was with rope because they forgot to bring their toys. They have some toys, but you can't play with them in these games. Next they were going to skip rope, and so the mother bear and the father bear held the end of the rope. Then baby bear jumped.   Then it was the papa bear's turn and it was the mother bear's turn, and then it went around and around. Then the baby bear said, "I want to play another game."   And then the baby bear asked before they started to play that game, "Who won?" And then the bear said, "I think you won, little one." And then next they were going to play "make a basket," and what they are going to do is cut the ropes, get some sticks, and start making out what they think will look like a basket. The end.

E: Ready for picture 3?

S: One day the lion was sitting in his big chair, and he was sitting there and he was bored. So he asked the little mouse, "Would you play a game with me?" And the mouse said, "Sure." So they played a game of marbles so the mouse wouldn't feel out of the game because he was so small. They played that for a while and then the lion said, "I'm getting tired of this game. Why don't we play tug-a-war?" So they got a little piece of string so the mouse could play, and they started tugging. The lion had fun with this for about 2 hours. Then he said, "Thank you, little mouse. I think I have some other ideas that one can play." So he started to play skipping rope, and he had fun with that. Then he sat in his big chair and took a nap. The end.

E: Ready for picture 4?

S: One day the kangaroo family was taking a picnic to the woods and the biggest was riding a bike. And the mother was going to the park for the picnic, and all the others—the two other kangaroos—thought that was a fine idea. So they went to the park, and then they sat down for a minute. Then they heard rattling in the woods that was by the park. So the mother said, "Wait right here. I'm going to go see what that was." When she was gone and it was quiet, someone came up and grabbed the two kangaroos that were sitting on the picnic quilt. And then he took them to a house, and it was a log house. And then the mother came back and she said, "Where is Fred, the biggest, and where is John, the littlest?" And so they went looking. Then the mother said, "I've heard of this kidnapper who's in the woods by the park, and he lives in a log cabin. So let's check there." So they went there and sure enough there they were. And she said, "I'm going to be going with my two children. Goodbye." The end.

E: This is card number 5.

S: One day the two little bears were sleeping one night. And then one woke up and woke the other up and said, "Let's talk." So they were whispering to each other. The time was about quarter 'til twelve, so they had slept a good while. And then their mama and papa bear were downstairs because they were getting a midnight snack. So the baby bear said, "Let's get out of our crib, and we'll go down and say hello to mama bear and papa bear." So they did just that. And then mama bear said, "You scurry up to bed now." So they went back to bed and they went to sleep. The end.

E: Card number 6.

S: Three bears were hibernating in a cave. And papa bear said, "I'm getting hungry." Of course, the other two were just sound asleep. So the papa bear said, "I'll go get some fish." So he went out and he got some fish and he ate the fish and said, "Those were so good." And he said, "How would you like me to get you a fish dinner tonight?" So the other two said, "Okay." Because they were so tired. So he went and got ten fish for the whole family. And he came back and he said, "These are the goodest I could get." So they said, "These are fine." So they were eating their dinner. And then he said, "I think when I finish dinner, I think I'm gonna go straight to bed." Of course it was winter time, and they had no place to walk around and go, so they just went back to sleep. And then someone knocked at the door, and so the papa bear answered it. It was the mail bear. And the mail bear said, "It's sure cold out there. I wondered if I could stay with you." They said, "Of course." And they had a happy night. The end.

E: Card number 7.

S: One night a tiger came after a monkey. And the tiger was really nice, but he thought the monkey was in his territory. So he went out after the monkey. And the monkey said, "Help!" But the lion said, " Well, you were in my territory." "Well, I didn't mean to Mr. Lion." So the tiger said to the monkey, "Okay, you can go now." So of course he was a very nice lion. And then he said, "I wonder what I can have for breakfast?" So (laughs) he went out to investigate for some deer that he could get. So he got an antelope instead of a deer because he gets confused of those two. So he ate that and said, "That's very good." So then he took an afternoon nap. Then he got up and said, "What's there to eat for lunch?" So he said, "I would like a monkey to eat."   (Laughs) This is really a strange lion. So he went out and got a monkey; it wasn't the monkey who trespassed, okay. So the tiger ate that monkey. Then he said, "I think I'm going to take a walk." So he took his walk, about 5 miles, because he needed to run. So he ran five mile each day. Then he said, "What is there to eat for dinner?" So he got out and said, "I think I'll eat. . . let's see, I think I'll go to town." And of course animals were in this town, since he was walking in a street-like jungle. So he went to town. "I think I'll try some food in the town." So he got a nice chicken dinner, and then he went to the candy shop and got some candy for dessert. The end.

E: This is card number 8.

S: The monkey family was talking and whispering, and they were having a pleasant time that afternoon. So then the baby monkey, or should I say child monkey, went out and he got his mother's permission. So he went out into the front yard, and he played and played and played. Then his friend came over and said, "Can I play with you?" "Did your mother say you could?" And the friend said, "No." Then the monkey said, "Well, go back and tell her that you're going to be over at my house for a few minutes and could you come play." So he checked out with his mother and his mother said, "Yes." Then he checked with his mother, and his mother said, "Okay." So they started to play tug-a-war. And then the monkey said, "I think I'll go in." So he went in and sat on the couch with his brother and sister. And his mother said, "Did you have fun?" Then he said, "Yes." And then he said, "Do you need to leave?" And the friend said, "No." And he said, "Come to my room and we'll play in there." So they started playing a battleship game. So the friend said, "I think I'll go now." The monkey went and ate dinner, and the monkey went to bed because he was really tired because his friend came over. The end.

LABORATORY REPORT FORM: CHILDREN'S APPERCEPTION TEST

Summarize:

	Story #1	Story #2
1. Main theme		
2. Main needs and drives of hero		
3. Conception of environment (world) as		
4. Parental figures are seen as ____________ Contemporary figures seen as ____________ Junior figures seen as ____________		
5. Significant conflicts		
6. Nature of anxieties		
7. Main defenses against conflicts and fears		
8. Adequacy of superego as manifested by "punishment" for crime being appropriate______ inappropriate______ too severe________ inconsistent______		
9. Integration of the ego, manifesting itself in Hero: adequate______ inadequate______ Outcome: happy______ unhappy______ realistic______ unrealistic______		

LABORATORY REPORT FORM: CHILDREN'S APPERCEPTION TEST

Summarize:

	Story #3	Story #4
1. Main theme		
2. Main needs and drives of hero		
3. Conception of environment (world) as		
4. Parental figures are seen as ____________ Contemporary figures seen as ____________ Junior figures seen as ____________		
5. Significant conflicts		
6. Nature of anxieties		
7. Main defenses against conflicts and fears		
8. Adequacy of superego as manifested by "punishment" for crime being appropriate______ inappropriate_____ too severe_______ inconsistent_____		
9. Integration of the ego, manifesting itself in Hero: adequate_____ inadequate____ Outcome: happy_____ unhappy_____ realistic____ unrealistic_____		

LABORATORY REPORT FORM: CHILDREN'S APPERCEPTION TEST – CONT.

Summary:

1.   What do the test responses reveal about this child?

2.   Discuss the relationship of psychoanalytic theory of personality development to the design of the test materials and the method of interpreting test responses.

3.   What is your opinion about this testing method and its usefulness in obtaining information about needs and drives?

Late Childhood

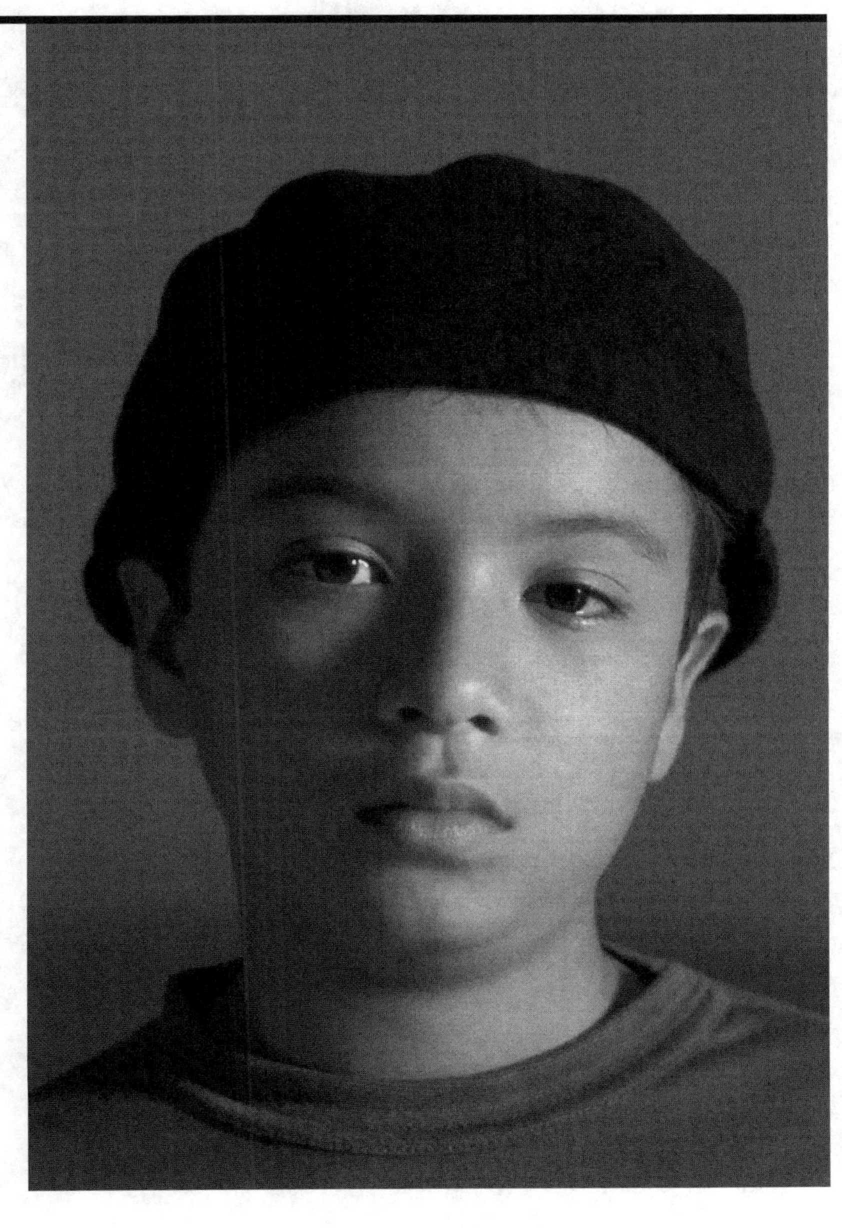

OBSERVATION: LATE CHILDHOOD

One of the best ways to learn about people is to observe them in the real world. This will give you the opportunity to see the full, genuine, and dynamic quality of human life across the life span.

Materials: Paper and pen for note-taking

Procedure: You will be observing people from **eight through eleven years of age**. You will be watching and recording behaviors. You are to observe each of the six stages of life span development for two hours, equaling a total of 12 hours for the entire semester. The two hour requirement for each stage does not have to be done in one sitting or with only one person. In fact, shorter segments with a variety of people are strongly encouraged so that you see individual differences as well as developmental similarities within the stage. The combinations need to total 2 hours. While observing, take notes and then consolidate your data into specific information for your paper. The format for this paper is described below.

A FEW HINTS FOR OBSERVING PEOPLE

1.   Be as unobtrusive as possible. You are entering the subjects' world so please do not disturb this world. Try to be objective.

2.   All you need is paper and pen to write down a few notes about the behavior and people you are observing. Do not take recorders or cameras. Do not write continually – observe, watch, listen.

3.   Write up your observation as soon as you finish observing while it is still fresh in your memory. Details are important. If you happen to know any of the subjects, do not use names when you write your observation.

4.   Observe in natural settings: parks, restaurants, malls, sports events, your front yard, schools, etc.

5.   Have the purpose of your research firmly in mind. Will you watch the entire playground or pick out one child to watch? Will you focus on one type of behavior or record all activities?

6.   Review developmental milestones from various theories before beginning your observation.

7.   Record verbal and nonverbal communication. Words, cries, screams, smiles, gestures, frowns, etc. all are important.

8.   If anyone asks what you are doing, be truthful.

OBSERVATION LATE CHILDHOOD – CONT.
FORMAT FOR THE OBSERVATION PAPER

Your paper must be typed, double-spaced, and a minimum of two pages in length. Indicate the location of the observation, the approximate age of subjects and the sex of subjects. The first section of the paper should be devoted to specific, objective behavioral data. The second section of the paper should emphasize the connections between your observations and developmental concepts from your text.

CONSERVATION

Conservation refers to the concept that changes in the appearance of substances do not necessarily mean changes in quantity of these substances. In the early childhood stage, most children do not grasp the concept of conservation. Usually around 7, conservation becomes a part of the cognitive concepts of a child.

Materials: string, clay, and pennies

Procedure: You will need to ask 2 children to help you in this experiment, one between 3 and 6 years of age and the other between 7 and 11 years of age. You will test these children on 3 separate common tasks: conservation of length, size, and number.

First, you will position the objects so that the child realizes they are equal. One of the objects will be changed as the child watches. Then you will ask the child if the objects are still equal despite the altered appearance. Finally, ask the child to explain his/her answer.

Do this procedure for each of the 3 tasks described on the following pages. Then repeat the entire process with the second child.

Answer the questions on your Laboratory Report Form(s).

LABORATORY REPORT FORM: CONSERVATION

1. Length

    A.   Cut 2 1/2 inch pieces of string and place them as pictured.

    B.   Ask the child if they are the same length and record your answer on your laboratory report form.

    C.   Rearrange the string as pictured

    D.   Ask the child if they are the same length. Record the answer.

    E.   Ask the child why and record the reason.

2. Size:

    A.   Take 2 equal balls of clay and place them as pictured.

    B.   Ask the child if they are the same size. Record the answer.

    C.   Reshape one ball as pictured.

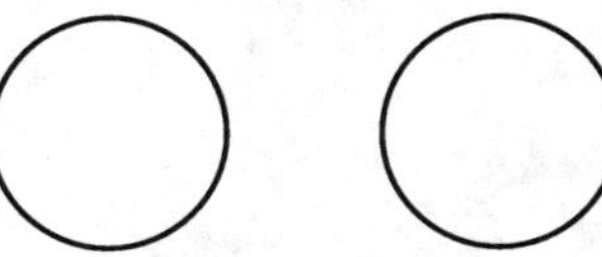

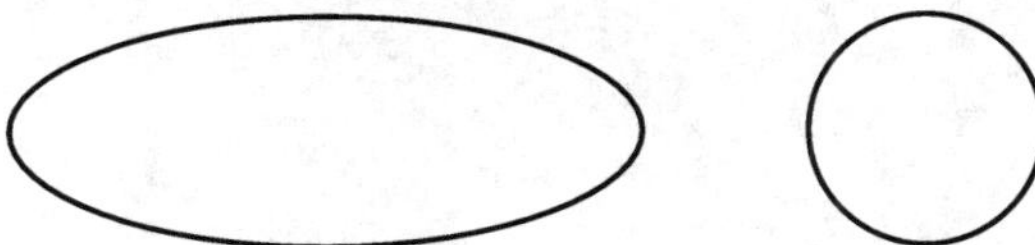

    D.   Ask the child if the 2 objects have the same amount of clay. Record the answer.

    E.   Ask why and record the reason.

LABORATORY REPORT FORM: CONSERVATION

3.   Number:

    A.   Place 2 rows of 10 pennies as pictured.

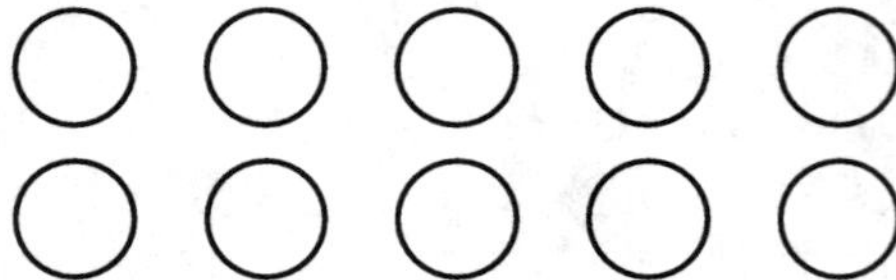

    B.   Ask the child if the same number of pennies is in each group. Record the answer.

    C.   Rearrange one group as pictured.

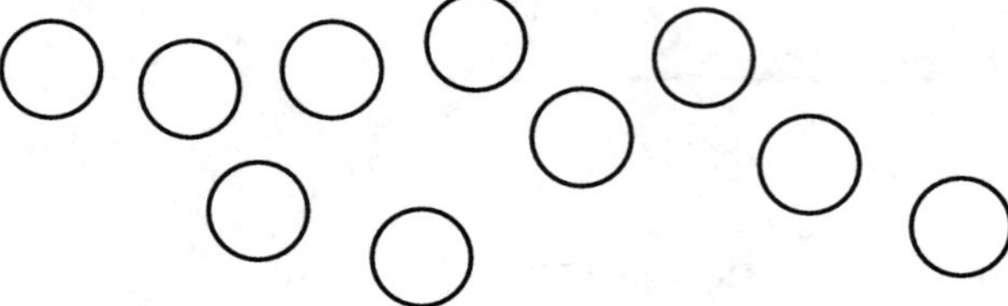

    D.   Ask the child if there is the same number of pennies in each group. Record the answer.

    E.   Ask the child why and record the reason.

LABORATORY REPORT FORM: CONSERVATION

Child #1   Age:__________

Task	**First Response**	**Altered Object Response**
Length	_________________________	_________________________
Size	_________________________	_________________________
Number	_________________________	_________________________

Child #2   Age:__________

Task	**First Response**	**Altered Object Response**
Length	_________________________	_________________________
Size	_________________________	_________________________
Number	_________________________	_________________________

Record exactly the response to "why" after the objects had been altered.

Task

Length   Child #1____

            Child #2____

Size   Child #1____

            Child #2____

Number   Child #1____

            Child #2____

Summary:

1.   Summarize your findings, describing differences in the performance of your two subjects.

HUMAN FIGURE DRAWING ANALYSIS

This assessment measures nonverbal cognitive maturity of children. Children's drawings follow sequential steps, which seem to follow certain maturational patterns, from the simple "tadpole" head and arms drawing to a well-defined, complete figure.

Use of children's drawings is intended to determine the level of understanding they have of their immediate world and themselves. The inclusion or exclusion of body parts is evaluated to determine this understanding. It is the extent of the child's cognitive development that determines what is important and what will be included or excluded from their drawings.

Materials: Human Figure Drawing Test

Procedure: Review the drawings provided by your instructor. Rate the drawings on the scoring sheet based on the scoring criteria. DO NOT ADMINISTER THIS TEST!

Answer the questions on your Laboratory Report Form(s).

Your instructor will give you the scoring criteria and explain the process for scoring and interpretation.

HUMAN FIGURE DRAWING TEST

SCORING FORM

1. _____ Head
2. _____ Head (Proportion)
3. _____ Eyes
4. _____ Eyes (Proportion)
5. _____ Pupils
6. _____ Lashes/Brows
7. _____ Nose
8. _____ Nose (Two dimensional)
9. _____ Nostrils
10. _____ Mouth
11. _____ Mouth (Two dimensional)
12. _____ Face (Proportion)
13. _____ Hair
14. _____ Neck
15. _____ Neck (Two dimensional)
16. _____ Trunk
17. _____ Trunk (Proportion)

18. _____ Shoulders
19. _____ Arms
20. _____ Arms (Two dimensional)
21. _____ Arms (Attachment)
22. _____ Arms (At side)
23. _____ Hands
24. _____ Fingers
25. _____ Fingers (Number)
26. _____ Fingers (Two dimensional)
27. _____ Thumb
28. _____ Legs
29. _____ Legs (Two dimensional)
30. _____ Legs (Proportion)
31. _____ Feet
32. _____ Feet (Two dimensional)
33. _____ Shoes
34. _____ Heel
35. _____ Total (Proportion)
36. _____ Total (Two dimensional)
37. _____ Clothing (1 item)
38. _____ Clothing (3 items)

______________ Raw Score

______________ IQ

______________ Percentile Ranking

LABORATORY REPORT FORM:
HUMAN FIGURE DRAWING ANALYSIS

1.   Name of child:

      Sex of child:

      Age of child:

2.   What did the results reveal about this child?

3.   Is this a valid test of intelligence? Support your conclusions with a detailed response.

4.   Do you agree or disagree with these results? Why?

TELEVISION ANALYSIS

Another element in society that greatly affects our personality development is television. In this experiment, you will be examining various children's television programs to study how these shows portray gender roles.

Materials: Children's television programs

Procedure: You are to watch 4 children's programs. Choose one of each from the following categories:

1. Traditional cartoons

2. Contemporary cartoons

3. Educational

4. Prime Time

Analyze each of these programs.

Answer the questions on your Laboratory Report Form(s).

LABORATORY REPORT FORM: TV ANALYSIS

Traditional Cartoon Title ____

1. How many male characters are portrayed?

2. How many female characters are portrayed?

3. What roles were portrayed by the males?

4. What roles were portrayed by the females?

5. How is masculinity portrayed both positively and negatively?

6. How is femininity portrayed both positively and negatively?

7. What is portrayed as appropriate female behavior?

8. What is portrayed as appropriate male behavior?

9.   How do women relate to each other and to men?

10.   How do men relate to each other and to women?

11.   How do men solve problems?

12.   How do women solve problems?

13.   What emotions do men experience?

14.   What emotions do women experience?

15.   Is there competition between people or cooperation for development of the individual?

16.   How many older adults were in the program? How were they portrayed?

17.   How many acts of violence did you see in this program?

LABORATORY REPORT FORM:
TV ANALYSIS

Contemporary Cartoon Title _______________________________

1.   How many male characters are portrayed?

2.   How many female characters are portrayed?

3.   What roles were portrayed by the males?

4.   What roles were portrayed by the females?

5.   How is masculinity portrayed both positively and negatively?

6.   How is femininity portrayed both positively and negatively?

7.   What is portrayed as appropriate female behavior?

8.   What is portrayed as appropriate male behavior?

9.   How do women relate to each other and to men?

10.   How do men relate to each other and to women?

11.   How do men solve problems?

12.   How do women solve problems?

13.   What emotions do men experience?

14.   What emotions do women experience?

15.   Is there competition between people or cooperation for development of the individual?

16.   How many older adults were in the program? How were they portrayed?

17.   How many acts of violence did you see in this program?

LABORATORY REPORT FORM:
TV ANALYSIS

Educational Title ____

1. How many male characters are portrayed?

2. How many female characters are portrayed?

3. What roles were portrayed by the males?

4. What roles were portrayed by the females?

5. How is masculinity portrayed both positively and negatively?

6. How is femininity portrayed both positively and negatively?

7. What is portrayed as appropriate female behavior?

8. What is portrayed as appropriate male behavior?

9.   How do women relate to each other and to men?

10.   How do men relate to each other and to women?

11.   How do men solve problems?

12.   How do women solve problems?

13.   What emotions do men experience?

14.   What emotions do women experience?

15.   Is there competition between people or cooperation for development of the individual?

16.   How many older adults were in the program? How were they portrayed?

17.   How many acts of violence did you see in this program?

LABORATORY REPORT FORM: TV ANALYSIS

Prime Time Title ____

1.   How many male characters are portrayed?

2.   How many female characters are portrayed?

3.   What roles were portrayed by the males?

4.   What roles were portrayed by the females?

5.   How is masculinity portrayed both positively and negatively?

6.   How is femininity portrayed both positively and negatively?

7.   What is portrayed as appropriate female behavior?

8.   What is portrayed as appropriate male behavior?

9.   How do women relate to each other and to men?

10.   How do men relate to each other and to women?

11.   How do men solve problems?

12.   How do women solve problems?

13.   What emotions do men experience?

14.   What emotions do women experience?

15.   Is there competition between people or cooperation for development of the individual?

16.   How many older adults were in the program? How were they portrayed?

17.   How many acts of violence did you see in this program?

LABORATORY REPORT FORM: TV ANALYSIS

Summary:

1. What characteristics did you discover about masculinity and femininity in the traditional cartoon?

    the contemporary cartoon?

    the educational program?

    the prime time program?

LABORATORY REPORT FORM: TV ANALYSIS

1.   Were there significant differences between these 4 categories? What were they?

2.   How does children's television portray men to young children?

3.   How does children's television portray women to young children?

4.   What did you discover about violence in children's television?

5.   How much effect do you think television has on the development of a child's personality?

Adolescence

OBSERVATION: ADOLESCENCE

One of the best ways to learn about people is to observe them in the real world. This will give you the opportunity to see the full, genuine, and dynamic quality of human life across the life span.

Materials: Paper and pen for note-taking

Procedure: You will be observing people from **twelve through twenty-two years of age**. You will be watching and recording behaviors. You are to observe each of the six stages of life span development for two hours, equaling a total of 12 hours for the entire semester. The two hour requirement for each stage does not have to be done in one sitting or with only one person. In fact, shorter segments with a variety of people are strongly encouraged so that you see individual differences as well as developmental similarities within the stage. The combinations need to total 2 hours. While observing, take notes and then consolidate your data into specific information for your paper. The format for this paper is described below.

A FEW HINTS FOR OBSERVING PEOPLE

1.   Be as unobtrusive as possible. You are entering the subjects' world so please do not disturb this world. Try to be objective.

2.   All you need is paper and pen to write down a few notes about the behavior and people you are observing. Do not take recorders or cameras. Do not write continually – observe, watch, listen.

3.   Write up your observation as soon as you finish observing while it is still fresh in your memory. Details are important. If you happen to know any of the subjects, do not use names when you write your observation.

4.   Observe in natural settings: parks, restaurants, malls, sports events, your front yard, schools, etc.

5.   Have the purpose of your research firmly in mind. Will you watch the entire playground or pick out one child to watch? Will you focus on one type of behavior or record all activities?

6.   Review developmental milestones from various theories before beginning your observation.

7.   Record verbal and nonverbal communication. Words, cries, screams, smiles, gestures, frowns, etc. all are important.

8.   If anyone asks what you are doing, be truthful.

OBSERVATION ADOLESCENCE – CONT.

FORMAT FOR THE OBSERVATION PAPER

Your paper must be typed, double-spaced, and a minimum of two pages in length. Indicate the location of the observation, the approximate age of subjects and the sex of subjects. The first section of the paper should be devoted to specific, objective behavioral data. The second section of the paper should emphasize the connections between your observations and developmental concepts from your text.

BODY IMAGE

During adolescence the individual goes through a process of re-establishing his/her self-concept involving a newly developed body. Much of the outcome of this re-evaluation process centers on cultural standards of beauty. These standards of beauty change so that the "ideal" body proportions and appearance are very different in 2006 from what they were in 1967.

In this research project you will be examining "ideal" appearances from various time periods.

Materials: Magazines, catalogs, books

Procedure: Locate pictures of paintings, sculptures, magazine illustrations, advertisements, or old snapshots from the following time periods that depict the standard of male or female beauty at that time:

1. **Late 1800's (1865 – 1900)**
2. **1930's**
3. **1950's**
4. **1970's**
5. **1990's – current**

Find at least 2 pictures from each period. Focus on either male or female images.

Attach your pictures to your Laboratory Report Form.

Answer the questions on your Laboratory Report Form(s).

LABORATORY REPORT FORM:
BODY IMAGE

1.   What similarities, if any, did you find across the 5 time periods?

2.   What was the key to having a "body beautiful" in the

Late 1800's

1930's

1950's

1970's

1990's – current

3.   During which time period do you think your body would have been the "ideal"? Why?

LABORATORY REPORT FORM: BODY IMAGE

4.   Based upon your research, do you believe that self-acceptance of body image is dependent upon societal ideals? Why?

5.   Can an individual change his/her body to match the society's "ideal"? To what extent?

6.   In your opinion, should an individual try to change his/her body strictly for image purposes? Why or why not?

7.   Do you see indications in our society today that self-acceptance is sometimes dependent upon things we cannot change? Give examples.

8.   What would you tell an adolescent who is struggling with this issue?

MOVIE ANALYSIS

Many adolescents spend a considerable amount of time "going to the movies." Certain movies depict some of the classic issues typical of the adolescent life span period of development: identity formation, formation of intimate friendships, esteem and belongingness needs, the significance of rites of passage, etc.

In this exercise you will be analyzing a feature-length movie and connecting the themes in the movie to certain developmental concepts.

Materials: Any "right of passage" movie approved by your instructor

Procedure: You are to view the movie.

Check with your instructor concerning availability of movie.

Answer the questions on your Laboratory Report Form(s).

LABORATORY REPORT FORM: MOVIE ANALYSIS

1.   How has each of the characters learned to cope with the stressors in his/her life?

2.   What developmental tasks from adolescence do you find displayed in the movie?

LABORATORY REPORT FORM:
MOVIE ANALYSIS

3.   How has each character strived to become an individual?

4.   What is it that brings the individuals together?

5.   How does each of the characters view him/herself and his/her world? Do these perceptions change any during the movie?

Early Adulthood

OBSERVATION: EARLY ADULTHOOD

One of the best ways to learn about people is to observe them in the real world. This will give you the opportunity to see the full, genuine, and dynamic quality of human life across the life span.

Materials: Paper and pen for note-taking

Procedure: You will be observing people from **23 through 40-45 years of age**. You will be watching and recording behaviors. You are to observe each of the six stages of life span development for two hours, equaling a total of 12 hours for the entire semester. The two hour requirement for each stage does not have to be done in one sitting or with only one person. In fact, shorter segments with a variety of people are strongly encouraged so that you see individual differences as well as developmental similarities within the stage. The combinations need to total 2 hours. While observing, take notes and then consolidate your data into specific information for your paper. The format for this paper is described below.

A FEW HINTS FOR OBSERVING PEOPLE

1. Be as unobtrusive as possible. You are entering the subjects' world so please do not disturb this world. Try to be objective.

2. All you need is paper and pen to write down a few notes about the behavior and people you are observing. Do not take recorders or cameras. Do not write continually – observe, watch, listen.

3. Write up your observation as soon as you finish observing while it is still fresh in your memory. Details are important. If you happen to know any of the subjects, do not use names when you write your observation.

4. Observe in natural settings: parks, restaurants, malls, sports events, your front yard, schools, etc.

5. Have the purpose of your research firmly in mind. Will you watch the entire playground or pick out one child to watch? Will you focus on one type of behavior or record all activities?

6. Review developmental milestones from various theories before beginning your observation.

7. Record verbal and nonverbal communication. Words, cries, screams, smiles, gestures, frowns, etc. all are important.

8. If anyone asks what you are doing, be truthful.

OBSERVATION EARLY ADULTHOOD – CONT.

FORMAT FOR THE OBSERVATION PAPER

Your paper must be typed, double-spaced, and a minimum of two pages in length. Indicate the location of the observation, the approximate age of subjects and the sex of subjects. The first section of the paper should be devoted to specific, objective behavioral data. The second section of the paper should emphasize the connections between your observations and developmental concepts from your text.

LIFE SCRIPT

Some psychologists consider early life experiences and family interaction patterns to be particularly significant in influencing our socioemotional development. This experiment involves your looking back at specific elements of your childhood and reflecting on the effects these factors have had on your becoming the person you are today.

Materials: Laboratory Report Forms

Procedure: Answer the questions on your Laboratory Report Forms and write a one page summary indicating which factors were most important in shaping your development.

LABORATORY REPORT FORM: LIFE SCRIPT

1.   What kind of person are you?

2.   What kind of person was your mother?

3.   What kind of person was your father?

4.   Did any other adults live in your home before you were 10 years old? (If yes, briefly describe each of them).

5.   What was your mother's favorite saying about life?

6.   How did your mother praise you – what did she say?

7.   How did your mother criticize you – what did she say?

8.   When your mother was upset, how did she show it?

9.   What did you do to help when your mother was upset?

10.   What was her advice to you as a child?

LABORATORY REPORT FORM: LIFE SCRIPT

11.   What was your father's favorite saying about life?

12.   How did your father praise you – what did he say?

13.   How did your father criticize you – what did he say?

14.   When your father was upset, how did he show it?

15.   What did you do to help when your father was upset?

16.   What was his advice to you as a child?

17.   When you were punished, what was mild and what was severe?

18.   Which punishment was most common?

19.   What nicknames have you had? What did they mean?

20.   Briefly describe how grown-ups talked to you as a child.

LABORATORY REPORT FORM: LIFE SCRIPT

21. What did your mother hope you would be?

22. What did your father hope you would be?

23. Are you closer to what your mother wanted or what your father wanted?

24. What feelings, thoughts, or attitudes were you not to reveal in your childhood?

25. What do you now say and believe about life?

26. What did you say and believe about life as a teenager?

27. What did you say and believe about life when you were in grade school?

28. What did you say and believe about life before you started school?

29. What do you like most about yourself?

30. What do you dislike about yourself?

LABORATORY REPORT FORM: LIFE SCRIPT

31.   What childhood stories did you like best?

32.   What person in the story did you like best and what did you like about the person?

33.   If someone disagrees with you, do you generally argue or give in?

34.   What would you have written on your tombstone?

35.   What might others have written on your tombstone?

36.   How do you wish your father might have been different?

37.   How do you wish your mother might have been different?

38.   If you were given wishes, what or how would you change?

39.   What do you most want in life?

LABORATORY REPORT FORM:
LIFE SCRIPT

Summary:

After answering these questions, think about your response to question #1. Which factors were most significant in shaping your development? Please explain, writing a response at least one page in length.

HOW SHY ARE YOU?

Research shows that most people believe they are shy and their shyness prevents them from being as happy as they would like to be. When shyness becomes a predominate characteristic, it can influence people to avoid social functions (e.g. parties) and to feel distressed about their inability to express themselves in a more outgoing manner. Does shyness create such problems for you?

By answering Watson's and Friend's "Social Avoidance and Distress Scale" below, you can obtain a quantitative measure of how shy you really are. (NOTE: This test is not meant to provide a professional diagnosis)

Materials: Measurement of Social-Evaluative Anxiety below.

Procedure: Beside each statement, put a (T) for True or an (F) for False.

_______   1.   I feel relaxed even in unfamiliar social situations.

_______   2.   I try to avoid situations which force me to be very sociable.

_______   3.   It is easy for me to relax when I am with strangers.

_______   4.   I have no particular desire to avoid people.

_______   5.   I often find social occasions upsetting.

_______   6.   I usually feel calm and comfortable at social occasions.

_______   7.   I am usually at ease when talking to people unless I know them well.

_______   8.   I try to avoid talking to people unless I know them well.

_______   9.   If the chance comes to meet new people, I often take it.

_______   10. I often feel nervous or tense in casual a get together in which both sexes are present.

_______   11. I am usually nervous with people unless I know them well.

_______   12. I usually feel relaxed when I am with a group of people.

_______   13. I often want to get away from people.

_______   14. I usually feel uncomfortable when I am in a group of people I don't know.

_______   15. I usually feel relaxed when I meet someone for the first time.

_______   16. Being introduced to people makes me tense and nervous.

_______   17. Even though a room is full of strangers, I may enter it anyway.

_______   18. I would avoid walking up and joining a large group of people.

HOW SHY ARE YOU? – CONT.

______   19. When my superiors want to talk with me, I talk willingly.

______   20. I often feel on edge when I am with a group of people.

______   21. I tend to withdraw from people.

______   22. I don't mind talking to people at parties or social gatherings.

______   23. I am seldom at ease in a large group of people.

______   24. I often think up excuses in order to avoid social engagements.

______   25. I sometimes take the responsibility for introducing people to each other.

______   26. I try to avoid formal social occasions.

______   27. I usually go to whatever social engagements I have.

______   28. I find it easy to relax with other people.

Summary:

1.   Which aspects of shyness present important problems for you? Why?

2.   How does shyness affect you? Why is it that some people just barely manage to cope with shyness while others successfully overcome their shyness?

3.   Did this test correctly measure your level of perceived shyness? What are some of the limitations of an objective pen and paper test in measuring vague emotional states?

ANDROGYNY

Androgyny refers to the capacity of men and women to be both masculine and feminine in their attitudes and behavior. For example a person can be both tough and tender, compassionate and strong, ambitious and sensitive to the needs of others. A person who successfully integrates both traditional male and female gender roles is said to be androgynous.

There is a great deal of debate among psychologists as to whether androgyny should be the goal of personality development in all individuals. Most research points out that androgynous individuals do seem to adapt more quickly and successfully, but androgyny does not solve all problems or guarantee more perfect relationships.

In this study you will explore androgyny on a personal level.

Materials: Androgyny Scale

Procedure: Upon completion of the inventory you will be given instructions on how to score the inventory and how to interpret these results.

Answer the questions on your Laboratory Report Form(s).

ANDROGYNY SCALE

Listed below are a number of personality characteristics. Use these to describe yourself. On the Androgyny Scale Scoring Form, indicate a scale of 1 to 5, how true of you these characteristics are. Do not leave any unmarked.

Column A	Column B	Column C
1. independent	2. dependable	3. productive
4. logical	5. obliging	6. commiserating
7. defends own beliefs	8. envious	9. merry
10. has leadership abilities	11. temperamental	12. sensitive to the needs of others
13. autonomous	14. honest	15. bashful
16. willing to take chances	17. scrupulous	18. sympathetic
19. robust	20. reticent	21. loving
22. makes decisions easily	23. dramatic	24. tender
25. confident	26. genuine	27. flatterable
28. cheerful	29. self-sufficient personality	30. powerful
31. eager to soothe hurt feelings	32. faithful	33. self-important
34. unpredictable	35. controlling	36. commanding
37. soft-spoken	38. feminine	39. amiable
40. versatile	41. masculine	42. individualistic
43. gracious	44. does not use harsh language	45. grave
46. unsystematic	47. willing to take a stand	48. competitive
49. kindhearted	50. loves children	51. sociable
52. tactful	53. aggressive	54. aspiring
55. trusting	56. gentle	57. inefficient
58. traditional	59. acts as a leader	60. childlike

ANDROGYNY SCALE SCORING FORM

1	2	3	4	5
never true	sometimes true	occasionally true	often true	always true

Column A	**Column B**	**Column C**
1. 1 2 3 4 5	2. 1 2 3 4 5	3. 1 2 3 4 5
4. 1 2 3 4 5	5. 1 2 3 4 5	6. 1 2 3 4 5
7. 1 2 3 4 5	8. 1 2 3 4 5	9. 1 2 3 4 5
10. 1 2 3 4 5	11. 1 2 3 4 5	12. 1 2 3 4 5
13. 1 2 3 4 5	14. 1 2 3 4 5	15. 1 2 3 4 5
16. 1 2 3 4 5	17. 1 2 3 4 5	18. 1 2 3 4 5
19. 1 2 3 4 5	20. 1 2 3 4 5	21. 1 2 3 4 5
22. 1 2 3 4 5	23. 1 2 3 4 5	24. 1 2 3 4 5
25. 1 2 3 4 5	26. 1 2 3 4 5	27. 1 2 3 4 5
28. 1 2 3 4 5	29. 1 2 3 4 5	30. 1 2 3 4 5
31. 1 2 3 4 5	32. 1 2 3 4 5	33. 1 2 3 4 5
34. 1 2 3 4 5	35. 1 2 3 4 5	36. 1 2 3 4 5
37. 1 2 3 4 5	38. 1 2 3 4 5	39. 1 2 3 4 5
40. 1 2 3 4 5	41. 1 2 3 4 5	42. 1 2 3 4 5
43. 1 2 3 4 5	44. 1 2 3 4 5	45. 1 2 3 4 5
46. 1 2 3 4 5	47. 1 2 3 4 5	48. 1 2 3 4 5
49. 1 2 3 4 5	50. 1 2 3 4 5	51. 1 2 3 4 5
52. 1 2 3 4 5	53. 1 2 3 4 5	54. 1 2 3 4 5
55. 1 2 3 4 5	56. 1 2 3 4 5	57. 1 2 3 4 5
58. 1 2 3 4 5	59. 1 2 3 4 5	60. 1 2 3 4 5

A = ____________   B = ____________

ANDROGYNY SCALE
Scoring Instructions

Of the preceding 60 personality characteristics listed, 20 are commonly thought of as masculine (ambitious, assertive, independent, etc.), 20 are feminine (affectionate, gentle, understanding, etc.), and 20 are neutral (truthful, likable, etc.). On the basis of your answers, you are to receive three major scores: a Masculinity Score, a Femininity Score, and an Androgyny score. To compute the Masculinity Score, add up all of the points in column A. Divide that sum by 20. To compute the Femininity score, add up all of the points in column B. Divide that sum by 20. If your Masculinity Score is above 3.5 and your Femininity Score is above 3.5, then you would be classified as Androgynous on Bem's Scale.

Scoring:

Column A = ________________ divided by 20 = _______ Masculinity score

Column B = ________________ divided by 20 = _______ Femininity score

To be Androgynous:
      the Masculinity score must be greater than 3.5
      or the Femininity score must be greater than 3.5

LABORATORY REPORT FORM: ANDROGYNY

Summary:

1.   What does your score mean?

2.   Were you surprised with these results? Why?

3.   Examine the personality characteristics. Do you agree with Dr. Bem on the labeling of certain characteristics as masculine or feminine?

4.   Give specific examples to substantiate your answer to question 3.

CAREER DECISION MAKING

Psychologists have developed many tests to help people find the right career. Most of these assessment tools involve matching your personality and interests with a career and then evaluating the opportunities and educational requirement for those fields.

In this exercise you will experience one of these assessment tools.

Materials: Career Assessment Inventories

Procedure: Go to the Career Services Office and make an appointment with a career counselor. They will give you further instructions. You may also want to schedule a follow up meeting for further elaboration of your assessment results.

Answer the questions on your Laboratory Report Form(s).

LABORATORY REPORT FORM:
CAREER DECISION MAKING

Summary:

1. What assessment tool did you choose and what were some of the results?

2. Do you agree or disagree with these results? Why?

3. What are your career goals?

4. What courses of action do you need to take to achieve these goals?

5. What kind of opportunities are available in these fields? (You may need some additional assistance from advisors in career planning or faculty members. ASK!!!)

Middle Adulthood

OBSERVATION: MIDDLE ADULTHOOD

One of the best ways to learn about people is to observe them in the real world. This will give you the opportunity to see the full, genuine, and dynamic quality of human life across the life span.

Materials: Paper and pen for note-taking

Procedure: You will be observing people from **46 through 65 years of age**. You will be watching and recording behaviors. You are to observe each of the six stages of life span development for two hours, equaling a total of 12 hours for the entire semester. The two hour requirement for each stage does not have to be done in one sitting or with only one person. In fact, shorter segments with a variety of people are strongly encouraged so that you see individual differences as well as developmental similarities within the stage. The combinations need to total 2 hours. While observing, take notes and then consolidate your data into specific information for your paper. The format for this paper is described below.

A FEW HINTS FOR OBSERVING PEOPLE

1. Be as unobtrusive as possible. You are entering the subjects' world so please do not disturb this world. Try to be objective.

2. All you need is paper and pen to write down a few notes about the behavior and people you are observing. Do not take recorders or cameras. Do not write continually – observe, watch, listen.

3. Write up your observation as soon as you finish observing while it is still fresh in your memory. Details are important. If you happen to know any of the subjects, do not use names when you write your observation.

4. Observe in natural settings: parks, restaurants, malls, sports events, your front yard, schools, etc.

5. Have the purpose of your research firmly in mind. Will you watch the entire playground or pick out one child to watch? Will you focus on one type of behavior or record all activities?

6. Review developmental milestones from various theories before beginning your observation.

7. Record verbal and nonverbal communication. Words, cries, screams, smiles, gestures, frowns, etc. all are important.

8. If anyone asks what you are doing, be truthful.

OBSERVATION MIDDLE ADULTHOOD – CONT.
FORMAT FOR THE OBSERVATION PAPER

Your paper must be typed, double-spaced, and a minimum of two pages in length. Indicate the location of the observation, the approximate age of subjects and the sex of subjects. The first section of the paper should be devoted to specific, objective behavioral data. The second section of the paper should emphasize the connections between your observations and developmental concepts from your text.

CASE STUDY

Case studies are in-depth studies of individuals that can often provide suggestions for further research. In this group activity you will be responsible for the development of a hypothetical case study involving midlife issues. Proposing solutions to problems, and surveying other groups regarding case dilemmas will also be a focus of this exercise.

Materials: None

Procedure: Small groups will be formed.

1. Select a topic of interest for <u>case study development</u> (e.g. physical changes, communication problems with adolescent children, job crisis, sexual dilemmas, marital relationship, etc.)

2. Focus on just one central problem or midlife dilemma and agree on your case study format.

3. Compose your case study, making it interesting and consistent with information presented in the text and in class.

4. As a group, generate as many potential solutions as you can for the problem you have described.

5. Rank your group's solution from most to least favorable.

6. Decide on a few different target groups to interview concerning the case (e.g. teenage child of midlife parent, clergy, males/females, young/old, persons from various race or socioeconomic statuses).

7. Each group member interviews a small sample from one target group. Show them your written case and ask for their preferred solution(s) to the dilemma presented. Then ask them to rank your group's potential solutions.

8. Reconvene to discuss and integrate the findings from your own solutions and the survey results from the various target groups. <u>Write a summary</u>.

9. Present your case study and findings to the class.

CAREER SATISFACTION SURVEY

During early adulthood, one of the important tasks most people accomplish is choosing a career. As adults continue to grow and develop, they evaluate and re-evaluate their attitudes toward their career choice. During the middle adulthood stage, some people change careers due to midlife re-evaluation resulting from low job satisfaction.

Materials: Laboratory Report Forms

Procedure: You are to ask 5 adults in various jobs or careers to complete the following questionnaire. You may ask each person to fill out the form, or you may conduct an interview with each subject. In either case, include the completed questionnaires (copy as needed) with your laboratory report form.

Answer the questions on your Laboratory Report Form(s).

LABORATORY REPORT FORM: CAREER SATISFACTION

Subject: Age________________   Gender__________________

1.   What do you consider to be the three most important characteristics of a satisfying career?
      (rank in order)

      a.

      b.

      c.

      Are there other characteristics you think are important? If so, which ones?

2.   What characteristics of a job or career would turn you away from that profession?

      a.

      b.

      c.

3.   What would be, for you, the ultimate career or occupation? Explain why.

LABORATORY REPORT FORM: CAREER SATISFACTION

4.   Is your ultimate career the career you have now?

     If not, how much does your current occupation relate to your ultimate career?

     If it does not relate at all, explain why you have not pursued your ultimate career occupation.

5.   How important is your career in achieving overall happiness and satisfaction in life (in general)? Explain your answer.

6.   What advice do you have for college students currently in the process of choosing an occupation?

LABORATORY REPORT FORM: CAREER SATISFACTION
Summary:

1.   According to your research, what factors seem most important to career satisfaction?

2.   In general, how did your subjects perceive the significance of career satisfaction in achieving overall life satisfaction?

3.   What factors contributed most to career dissatisfaction?

BASIC LIFE EXPECTANCY

This assessment will tell you your approximate life expectancy and will delineate those factors in your life which are contributing to or subtracting from longevity.

Materials: Laboratory Report Forms

Procedure: Decide how each item below applies to you and add or subtract the appropriate number of years from your basic life expectancy (average male life expectancy = 70; average female life expectancy = 75).

Answer the summary questions on your laboratory report form(s).

LABORATORY REPORT FORM:
BASIC LIFE EXPECTANCY

1.   Family history
     Add five years if two or more of your grandparents live to
     80 or beyond.   ________
     Subtract four years if any parent, grandparent, sister, or
     brother died of heart attack or stroke before 50.   ________
     Subtract two years if anyone died from these diseases
     before 60.   ________
     Subtract three years for each case of diabetes, thyroid
     disorder, breast cancer, cancer of the digestive system,
     asthma, or chronic bronchitis among parents or grandparents.   ________

2.   Marital status
     If you are married, add four years.   ________
     If you are over twenty-five and not married, subtract one
     year for every unwedded decade.   ________

3.   Economic status
     Add two years if your family income is over $60,000
     per year.   ________
     Subtract three years if you have been poor for the greater
     part of your life.   ________

4.   Physique
     Subtract one year for every ten pounds you are overweight.   ________
     For each inch your girth measurement exceeds
     your chest measurement, deduct two years.   ________
     Add three years if you are over forty and not overweight.   ________

5.   Exercise
     Add three years if you exercise regularly and
     moderately (jogging three times a week).   ________
     Add five years if you exercise regularly and
     vigorously (long-distance running three times a week.)   ________
     Subtract three years if your job is sedentary   ________
     Add three years if your job is active.   ________

6.   Alcohol
     Add two years if you are a light drinker
     (one or three drinks a week).   ________
     Subtract one year if you are a teetotaler.   ________

LABORATORY REPORT FORM: BASIC LIFE EXPECTANCY

7. Smoking
    Subtract eight years if you smoke two or
    more packs of cigarettes per day.   _________
    Subtract two years if you smoke one to two
    packs per day.   _________
    Subtract two years if you smoke less than
    one pack.   _________
    Subtract two years if you regularly smoke
    a pipe or cigars.   _________
                                                           ____

8. Disposition
    Add two years if you a reasoned, practical
    person.   _________
    Subtract two years if you are aggressive,
    intense, and competitive.   _________
    Add one to five years if you are basically
    and content with life.   _________
    Subtract one to five years if you are often
    unhappy, worried, and often feel guilty.   _________

9. Education
    Subtract two years if you have less than a
    high school education.   _________
    Add one year if you attended four years of
    school beyond high school.   _________
    Add three years if you attended five or more
    years beyond high school.   _________

10. Environment
    Add four years if you have lived most of
    your life in a rural environment.   _________
    Subtract two years if you have lived most
    of your life in an urban environment.   _________

11. Sleep
    Subtract five years if you sleep more than
    nine hours a day.   _________

12. Temperature
    Add two years if your home's thermostat is
    set at no more than 68 F.   _________

13. Health Care
    Add three years if you have regular medical
    checkups and regular dental care.   _________
    Subtract two years if you are frequently
    ill.   _________
Your Life Expectancy Total   _________

LABORATORY REPORT FORM: BASIC LIFE EXPECTANCY

Average male life expectancy = 70

Average female life expectancy = 75

Write down your average life expectancy based totally upon whether you are male or female.

_____________ years average life expectancy.

+ 10 yrs. if you are in your 50's or 60's

+ 2 yrs. if you are over 60

_____________ yrs. subtotal

Now use this subtotal to add or subtract the points on this test.

Your life expectancy ___________ yrs.

Summary:

1.   What factors are adding to your longevity?

2.   What factors are subtracting years?

3.   Which of these factors surprised or concerned you? Why?

Late Adulthood

OBSERVATION: LATE ADULTHOOD

One of the best ways to learn about people is to observe them in the real world. This will give you the opportunity to see the full, genuine, and dynamic quality of human life across the life span.

Materials: Paper and pen for note-taking

Procedure: You will be observing people from **65+ years of age**. You will be watching and recording behaviors. You are to observe each of the six stages of life span development for two hours, equaling a total of 12 hours for the entire semester. The two hour requirement for each stage does not have to be done in one sitting or with only one person. In fact, shorter segments with a variety of people are strongly encouraged so that you see individual differences as well as developmental similarities within the stage. The combinations need to total 2 hours. While observing, take notes and then consolidate your data into specific information for your paper. The format for this paper is described below.

A FEW HINTS FOR OBSERVING PEOPLE

1.   Be as unobtrusive as possible. You are entering the subjects' world so please do not disturb this world. Try to be objective.

2.   All you need is paper and pen to write down a few notes about the behavior and people you are observing. Do not take recorders or cameras. Do not write continually – observe, watch, listen.

3.   Write up your observation as soon as you finish observing while it is still fresh in your memory. Details are important. If you happen to know any of the subjects, do not use names when you write your observation.

4.   Observe in natural settings: parks, restaurants, malls, sports events, your front yard, schools, etc.

5.   Have the purpose of your research firmly in mind. Will you watch the entire playground or pick out one child to watch? Will you focus on one type of behavior or record all activities?

6.   Review developmental milestones from various theories before beginning your observation.

7.   Record verbal and nonverbal communication. Words, cries, screams, smiles, gestures, frowns, etc. all are important.

8.   If anyone asks what you are doing, be truthful.

OBSERVATION LATE ADULTHOOD – CONT.
FORMAT FOR THE OBSERVATION PAPER

Your paper must be typed, double-spaced, and a minimum of two pages in length. Indicate the location of the observation, the approximate age of subjects and the sex of subjects. The first section of the paper should be devoted to specific, objective behavioral data. The second section of the paper should emphasize the connections between your observations and developmental concepts from your text.

MISCONCEPTIONS OF OLD AGE

The percentage of older people in the U.S. population is increasing rapidly; it is estimated by the year 2030 more than 65 million Americans (25% of the population) will be 65 or older. Accompanying this increase has been more research on the aging process and its effects on the individual.

Many students enter the classroom with perceptions of "old age" resulting from information obtained from books/magazines, television, radio, or other forms of popular media. Often, this knowledge creates beliefs which are at odds with scientific research.

Materials: Questionnaire below

Procedure: Answer the ten true/false questions and score your paper according to the answer sheet provided by the instructor.

_____ 1.   If people live long enough, they will become senile.

_____ 2.   As older adults grow older, they become more alike.

_____ 3.   Old age is generally a time of serenity.

_____ 4.   Older people tend to show little interest in sex.

_____ 5.   Older adults tend to be inflexible.

_____ 6.   Most older people lack creativity and are unproductive.

_____ 7.   Older people have great difficulty in learning new skills.

_____ 8.   When people grow old, they generally become "cranky."

_____ 9.   Most older people are lonely and isolated.

_____ 10.   As people become older, they are likely to become more religious.

Comments:

LABORATORY REPORT FORM: MISCONCEPTIONS OF OLD AGE

Summary:

1.   What did this test reveal regarding your own misconceptions of old age?

2.   What sources of information have influenced your beliefs about old age?

3.   Based on your reading and class discussions, describe the scientific findings regarding old age that surprise you the most.

SENSORY LOSSES SIMULATION

Predictable physical changes occur with advancing age. It is often difficult to appreciate or understand the sensory losses that sometimes accompany aging. For example, many older individuals must contend with impaired vision and hearing. Normal physical decline does not necessarily mean that the elderly are unable to take care of their houses, do yard work, or play tennis. On the contrary, most activities can still be carried out just as effectively and enjoyably although they may take longer. This exercise was designed to help you better understand sensory losses many adults experience in late adulthood.

Materials: Masking Tape
Cotton balls
Plastic wrap

Procedure: First, wrap the masking tape around the knuckles on your dominant hand. This depicts the stiffness caused by arthritis. Next, try to write your name without breaking the tape.

Second, put cotton balls in your ears. This represents what the world sounds like when hearing loss occurs. Continue to listen to the lecture and/or instructions being given by the instructor.

Third, place the plastic wrap around your eyes. This simulates cataracts. Now, write your name again. Take off the plastic wrap and view your writings.

Answer the questions on your Laboratory Report Form(s).

LABORATORY REPORT FORM:
SENSORY LOSSES SIMULATION

Summary:

1. What did your handwriting look like after you wrote your name with the masking tape around your knuckles? How did you feel?

2. When you put the cotton balls in your ears, what happened to the sounds around you? When asked if you could hear okay by the instructor, what did you say? How did you feel?

3. After putting plastic wrap around your eyes, how could you see? What did your name look like this time? How did you feel?

4. "Ageism" occurs when elderly people are viewed in a negative light by society. Reflect upon each aspect of this experiment and indicate why the elderly may not want to admit any one of these sensory losses.

ALTERNATIVE HOUSING

One of the major decisions older adults tend to wrestle with is where to live. As children leave home the larger house is no longer needed. Many older adults want to spend much of their year traveling or involved in other leisure activities now that they have increased freedom from responsibilities. Also, the issue of decreasing health or death of a spouse faces many older adults. All of these issues contribute to the dilemma of where to live.

In this exercise you will be examining several options of living arrangements for "senior citizens.

Materials: Laboratory Report Forms

Procedure: You are to visit or telephone 3 different types of housing facilities for senior citizens in your county. Fill in the Laboratory Report Forms for each facility.

Your options include: retirement communities, nursing homes, senior citizens centers, private individual homes, living with children or other relatives, and apartment complexes.

Answer the questions on your Laboratory Report Form(s).

LABORATORY REPORT FORM: ALTERNATIVE HOUSING

Alternative #1 ____

1.   What type of housing?

2.   What is the cost per month?

3.   What special services are offered?

      Medical

      Economic

      Intellectual

      Meals

4.   Do these services cost extra?

5.   At what age is a person eligible to live at this particular facility?

6.   What type of staffing does the housing complex employ?

7.   Is this facility approved for Medicare/Medicaid or insurance reimbursement?

8.   Any additional comments or observations.

LABORATORY REPORT FORM: ALTERNATIVE HOUSING

Alternative #2 ______________________________________

1.   What type of housing?

2.   What is the cost per month?

3.   What special services are offered?

Medical

Economic

Intellectual

Meals

4.   Do these services cost extra?

5.   At what age is a person eligible to live at this particular facility?

6.   What type of staffing does the housing complex employ?

7.   Is this facility approved for Medicare/Medicaid or insurance reimbursement?

8.   Any additional comments or observations.

LABORATORY REPORT FORM: ALTERNATIVE HOUSING

Alternative #3 ____

1.   What type of housing?

2.   What is the cost per month?

3.   What special services are offered?

Medical

Economic

Intellectual

Meals

4.   Do these services cost extra?

5.   At what age is a person eligible to live at this particular facility?

6.   What type of staffing does the housing complex employ?

7.   Is this facility approved for Medicare/Medicaid or insurance reimbursement?

8.   Any additional comments or observations.

LABORATORY REPORT FORM: ALTERNATIVE HOUSING

Summary:

1.   Which situation, in your opinion, is the most favorable living alternative? Why?

2.   What were you surprised to learn about these alternatives? (e.g. cost, services, age requirements, etc.)

3.   How did this research affect your plans for your older adult years? As you plan for retirement what changes will you make based upon this research?

OBITUARY

During the late adulthood stage of development, Erikson theorized that adults confront the task of determining whether they are satisfied with having led an active, full, complete life or whether they have wasted their life. This integrity vs. despair dilemma greatly determines how a person will live and develop during this last stage of development. A person who feels successful faces their later years with optimism, enthusiasm and a new unification of personality. A person who feels despair tends to view this last stage of development with loss, disappointment, regret, and no purpose to live.

One of the ways to prepare for later adulthood is to live and enjoy each day of your life to the fullest, develop reasonable goals for your future, and develop an unconditional love for yourself and others.

In this experiment, you will attempt to understand yourself and your development a little more fully.

Materials: None

Procedure: You are to write two obituaries. The first obituary should be written as if you had just died.

The second obituary should be written as if you lived to be 87 years old. This, of course, will be speculative based on your current goals.

Your laboratory report form will help you organize your obituaries.

LABORATORY REPORT FORM: OBITUARY

Obituary #1 (if you had just died)

Full Name:

Date of Birth: Place of Birth:

Date of Death:

Survivors:

Accomplishments:

   (Education, Honors, Scholarships, Publications, Awards, Sports, etc.)

Profession:

Leisure Activities or Hobbies:

Contributions to the Community:

Membership in Professional, Community, and/or Religious Organizations.

LABORATORY REPORT FORM:
OBITUARY

Obituary #2 (87 years of age: if you are 20 it will be 67 years from today, if you are 30 it will be 57 years from today, etc.)

Full Name:

Date of Birth: Place of Birth:

Date of Death:

Survivors:

Accomplishments:

    (Education, Honors, Scholarships, Publications, Awards, Sports, etc.)

Profession:

Leisure Activities or Hobbies:

Contributions to the Community:

Membership in Professional, Community, and/or Religious Organizations.

THE SELF ACROSS THE LIFE SPAN

Developmental psychologists note the changes in the sense of self throughout the life span. This exercise allows you to interview individuals representing six of the life span periods and analyze the differences of sense of self.

Materials: None

Procedure: Interview six individuals, one each from early childhood, late childhood, adolescence, early adulthood, middle adulthood, and late adulthood. Simply ask each person to self-describe himself/herself. Ask, "Tell me who you are?" or "Tell me about you." Write down responses verbatim, and then analyze differences in perception of self throughout the life span based on these responses. Your analysis should be at least two pages, typed, and double-spaced. Include the six verbatim self-descriptions in your paper.

REFERENCES

Beers, Susan E. (1987). <u>Activities Handbook for the Teaching of Psychology</u>. Vol. 2: "Show and Tell" for Developmental Psychology, p. 93-94.

Bellak, Leopold. (1949). Children's Apperception Test. Western Psychological Services, Los Angeles, CA.

Bem, S.L. (1974). The Measurement of Psychological Androgyny. <u>Journal of Consulting and Clinical Psychology</u>. p. 42, 155-162.

Gardner, R.M. (1980). <u>Experiences in General Psychology</u>. Prentice-Hall: Englewood Cliffs, N.J.

Gonzales, Eloy (1986). Human Figure Drawing Test. Pro-ed, Austin, TX.

Holloway, William H. (1973). Life Script Questionnaire. Midwest Institute for Human Understanding, Inc., Medina, OH.

Schultz, Richard. (1978). Basic Life Expectancy. <u>The Psychology of Death, Dying, and Bereavement</u>. Newbery Records, Inc., division of Random House, Inc.

Shore, H. (1976). Designing a Training Program for Understanding Sensory Losses in Aging. <u>Gerontologist</u>, 16, p. 157-165.

Watson, D. and Friend, R. Measurement of Social-Evaluative Anxiety. <u>Journal of Consulting and Clinical Psychology</u>, 1969, Vol. 33, No. 4, 448-457.

Zimbardo, P.G. <u>Shyness</u>. New York: Harcourt Brace, 1978.